Heywood Brothers & Wakefield Company

CLASSIC WICKER FURNITURE

The Complete 1898–1899 Illustrated Catalog

With a New Introduction by
RICHARD SAUNDERS
Author of *Collecting and Restoring Wicker Furniture*

DOVER PUBLICATIONS, INC., NEW YORK

Published in Canada by General Publishing Company, Ltd., 30 Lesmill Road, Don Mills, Toronto, Ontario.
Published in the United Kingdom by Constable and Company, Ltd.

This Dover edition, first published in 1982, is a republication of the 1898–1899 catalog of the Heywood Brothers and Wakefield Company. Each page of the present edition contains two pages of the original. Color illustrations of the original are here reproduced on the covers. The thumb index and index by catalog numbers of the original are here omitted. Original pages 107–110 are rearranged for better page makeup. A new Introduction has been written especially for the Dover edition by Richard Saunders.

The publisher gratefully acknowledges the cooperation of the Eleutherian Mills Historical Library, Wilmington, Delaware, in making its copy of the catalog available for reproduction.

Manufactured in the United States of America
Dover Publications, Inc., 180 Varick Street, New York, N.Y. 10014

Library of Congress Cataloging in Publication Data

Heywood Brothers and Wakefield Company.
    Classic wicker furniture.

    Originally published: Reed & ratten furniture : Gardner?, Mass., Heywood Brothers and Wakefield Co., 1898–1899.
    1. Heywood Brothers and Wakefield Company—Catalogs.   2. Wicker furniture—Catalogs.
I. Title.
TS887.H48   1982   684.1'06   82-4583
ISBN 0-486-24355-9   AACR2

INTRODUCTION TO THE DOVER EDITION

On March 17, 1897, under the front-page headline "Two Large Firms to Merge," the *New York Times* reported: "The Wakefield Rattan Company will be merged with the firm of Heywood Brothers & Company, thus effecting one of the most important consolidations of capital yet made in New England." Less than a month after this article appeared, the two leading manufacturers of wicker furniture in the world were incorporated and formally joined forces to create the now-famous Heywood Brothers and Wakefield Company. The merger was a consolidation of furniture designers, master craftsmen and shrewd business minds from each company and not merely the "consolidation of capital" reported in the *Times*. Thus the first joint catalog of 1898–1899, reprinted here, in which each company contributed designs and shared in the actual labor, is of special significance. It is this catalog which marks the true beginning of the most famous of all wicker-furniture companies, for when these two giants of the industry combined forces they produced some of the finest handmade wicker furniture ever made. Not only a beautifully printed catalog, this initial collaboration between the two companies resulted in an extra treat for the public in the way of color illustrating the true tone of the "fancy colored reeds" referred to throughout this issue.* On this, the eighty-fifth anniversary of the formation of the Heywood Brothers and Wakefield Company, it seems fitting to bring back the premiere issue of this rare trade catalog—one that is painstakingly accurate in presenting the fantastic line of furniture which the company offered to the general public during the golden age of wicker.

While a large part of the public still clings to the misconception that most wicker furniture was made in the Orient, a growing awareness that this is an American-born industry is finally taking hold. Although wicker furniture actually dates back to ancient Egypt and was produced through the centuries out of necessity and from readily available materials, the "industry" per se has its roots in Boston. It was on the waterfront of this great city, in 1844, that an enterprising young grocer named Cyrus Wakefield happened to observe a huge quantity of rattan being dumped out on the docks after having served its purpose as dunnage aboard a clipper ship on its return voyage from the Far East. Fate seemed to take over from that point on; soon after examining one of the long, flexible poles, Wakefield decided that furniture could be made from this strange material. Although he had virtually no experience in this field, he began experimenting by making numerous pieces of crude rattan furniture during the next few years. Eventually he quit the grocery business and decided to import whole rattan from China to meet the growing demand in America for

split rattan or "cane" (the glossy, outer skin of the rattan vine which was employed in weaving chair seats). While building his jobbing trade Wakefield continued to experiment not only with rattan but with reed—the inner pith of the rattan vine which, up until that time, had always been treated as waste. He soon found that reed was more pliable than rattan and began stepping up his furniture-making experiments by using this newly discovered material. Finally, in the mid-1850s, he and his wife moved to South Reading, Massachusetts (later renamed "Wakefield" to honor the philanthropic endeavors of its most civic-minded citizen), where he quickly established the Wakefield Rattan Company.

Throughout the Civil War years Cyrus Wakefield continued to refine the art of making wicker furniture at affordable prices. By this time increasingly ornate Victorian designs (which were made possible by the use of the elastic-like reed) had become a sensation as porch and garden furniture. In the meantime one of the oldest furniture manufacturers in the United States, Heywood Brothers and Company (established in 1826), looked at the new wicker furniture industry with more than a passing interest and by the early 1870s began producing their own line of wicker products from their factory in Gardner, Massachusetts. Within a few years Levi Heywood, founder of the company, realized that wicker was more than a mere fad and stepped up production by adding such specialty items as perambulators, cribs and five-piece suites.

In 1873 Cyrus Wakefield died of a heart attack and his nephew and namesake, Cyrus Wakefield II, took over the management of the firm. By this time the Wakefield Rattan Company and Heywood Brothers and Company were the two leading manufacturers of wicker furniture in the country and proved to be intense rivals for a quarter of a century—a competitiveness that encouraged experimentation, improved existing designs and lowered prices. Strangely enough, the two companies had much in common: by the mid-1880s both firms were being managed by second generations (Henry Heywood took over as head of Heywood Brothers and Company when his uncle, Levi Heywood, died in 1882); their rates of growth during this period were remarkably similar; each firm employed Irish and Italian immigrants to fill their all-important labor forces and they were making closely related products toward the end of the nineteenth century.

When the two firms were finally incorporated in 1897, the newly formed Heywood Brothers and Wakefield Company was destined to all but monopolize the wicker-furniture industry. One of Henry Heywood's first acts as president was to establish two new warehouses in London and Liverpool, thereby creating an export market and ex-

*See the Note on the Dover Edition following this Introduction.

panding the total number of warehouses to eleven. This, coupled with the fact that the new company had huge factories in Gardner and Wakefield, Massachusetts, as well as Chicago and San Francisco, discouraged serious competition.

Although this was the first trade catalog to be issued by the Heywood Brothers and Wakefield Company, some older wicker designs can be found in the 1898 issue. For instance, the Lady's Reception Chair (number 6013 A, page 52)* and the Couch (number 6238, page 144) are representative of designs employed by each company during the 1880s, yet they were carried over into the 1898 joint catalog because they were exceptionally strong designs that had enjoyed healthy sales in earlier catalogs. In this way each company felt they were contributing their strongest designs at the time of the merger. On the other hand, some of the newer designs in the catalog, such as the Lady's Armchair (number 6545 A, page 25) and the Round Table (number 6377, page 174), caught on quickly and not only survived the turn of the century but were still being produced as late as the First World War.

The 1898 catalog opens, appropriately, with a long line of the most popular of all wicker items—the rocker. In the Lady's Rocking Chair (number 6092 B, page 6) we see the rolled serpentine arms and back, a design that began to appear in the 1880s and came into its own throughout the 1890s. A variation on the rocking-chair theme was the Lady's Comfort Patent Rocker (number 6315 BPR, page 30). Now called "platform rockers," these pieces were heavier than their traditional counterparts but required less room than a standard rocker since the powerful spring mechanism eliminated any drastic rocking motion.

While many of the designs employed in making the wicker armchairs (beginning on page 63) were also made as rocking chairs, some of the newer designs were merely awkward experiments and soon removed from the line. The Lady's Arm Chair (number 6509 A, page 73) and the Large Arm Chair (number 6512 C, page 87) are prime examples of this overindulgence. By contrast, the Large Arm Chair (number 6195 C, page 85) is a study in simplicity. This particular design (introduced by the Chinese at the 1876 Phila-

delphia Centennial Exhibition as the "hourglass chair" because of the hourglass design under the seat) is a variation on one of the few lasting designs in this field to come out of the Orient. The only other piece of wicker in the entire catalog that was not developed in America is the Beach Chair (page 109), which was actually based on a sixteenth-century French hooded wicker chair called a *guérite*.

Other chairs worthy of special attention in this section are the Morris Chair (number 6257, page 101) with its adjustable back, plush cushions and "Aladdin Slipper" legs; the unique square-backed Conversation Chair (number 6260, page 105); the Adult Cabinet Chair on page 108, intended for invalid use and very rare today; the Posing Chair on page 113, which is a good example of the "photographer's chairs" used as props in Victorian photography studios; and, finally, the Piano Chair (number 6372, page 117), complete with adjustable seat and wooden beads worked into the back.

While some of the newer designs offered variety, many of the established pieces (such as the Tete-a-Tete on page 133) can only be called classic in design. This also holds true for the Child's Table Chair (number 6310½ S, page 163), complete with wooden shelf; the Standing Crib on page 173; the Round Table (number 6409, page 180), illustrating the popular "birdcage" design at the bottom of the legs; the Music Stand (number 6440, page 199), which was used as the official logo for the newly formed company and appeared on each bill of sale; the Fancy Cabinet (number 6444, page 200); and the elaborate Dressing Stand which appears on page 201.

By the time the firm of Heywood Brothers and Wakefield Company was incorporated, the public had fully accepted wicker furniture on all fronts—the porch, the garden, the sitting room and the bedroom. Not only had wicker's three-dimensional, airy quality won the public over, but its sheer adaptability seemed to suit the age. If anything, this catalog should serve as a visual record of wicker furniture at its peak —both in popularity and in the superior hand-workmanship that is illustrated in the following pages.

Pacific Grove, California　　　　　　　　Richard Saunders
April, 1982

*All references are to the pages of the original edition, reproduced here two to a page (see the Note on the Dover Edition).

Note on the Dover Edition

In the present edition: (1) Each page, beginning with 2, represents two pages of the original catalog. Thus, Dover page 3, for instance, contains pages 5 and 6 of the original. This is reflected in the form of the folio numbering used herein, "[5 & 6] *3*" standing for "Dover page 3, containing original pages 5 and 6."

(2) The two color plates that originally appeared at the beginning of the catalogue are here reproduced as four separate color illustrations on the covers. These color pictures were referred to throughout the catalog by the phrase: "Fancy Colored Reeds Similar to Illustrations Shown in Front of Catalogue." For reasons of layout, the phrase is omitted from the present edition. Places where it occurred are marked by an asterisk (*).

ESTABLISHED 1826

1898-1899

INCORPORATED 1897

HEYWOOD BROTHERS AND WAKEFIELD COMPANY

MAKERS OF

REED AND RATTAN FURNITURE

CHAIRS, CHAIR CANE CHILDREN'S CARRIAGES

FACTORIES:

Gardner, Mass.

Chicago, Ill.

Wakefield, Mass.

San Francisco,

Cal.

WAREHOUSES:

NEW YORK, 195-197 CANAL ST.,

NEW YORK, 297-303 CHERRY ST.,

BOSTON, 182 PORTLAND ST.,

PHILADELPHIA, 1010-1014 RACE ST.,

BALTIMORE, 536-542 W. PRATT ST.,

CHICAGO, 270-272 WABASH AVE.,

SAN FRANCISCO, 659-663 MISSION ST.,

PORTLAND, ORE., 80-86 FIFTH ST.,

LOS ANGELES, 355-361 UPPER MAIN ST.,

LONDON, ENG., LIVERPOOL, ENG.

6085 B

Lady's Rocking Chair

6086 B

Lady's Rocking Chair

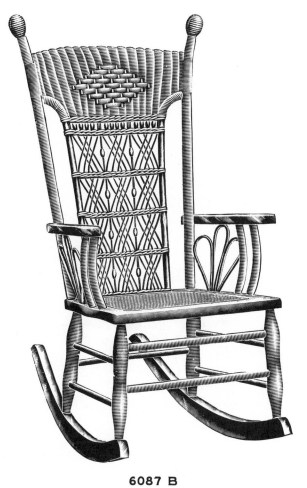

6087 B

Lady's Rocking Chair

6088 B

Lady's Rocking Chair *

6091 B

Lady's Rocking Chair

6092 B

Lady's Rocking Chair *

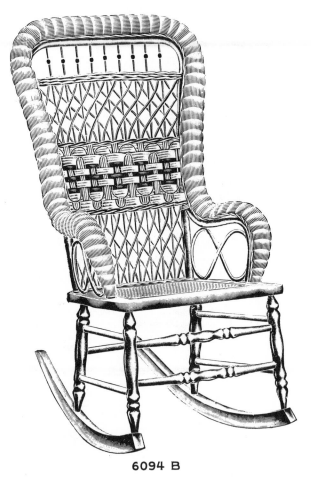

6094 B

Lady's Rocking Chair *

6096 B

Lady's Rocking Chair

6090 B

Lady's Rocking Chair *

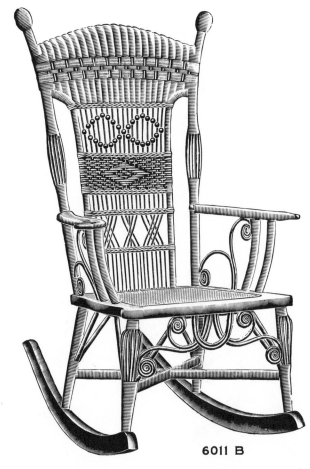

6011 B

Lady's Rocking Chair

6097 B

Lady's Rocking Chair

6098 B

Lady's Rocking Chair ⁕

6475 B

Lady's Rocking Chair ⁕

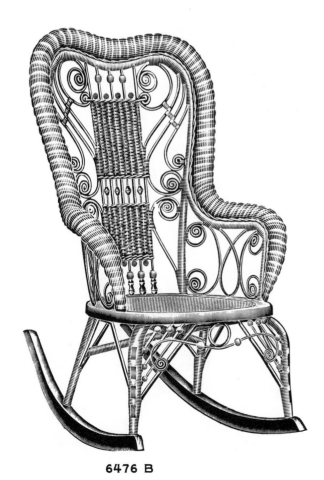

6476 B

Lady's Rocking Chair

[9 & 10] 5

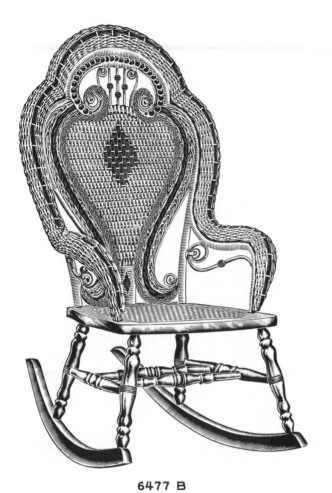

6477 B

Lady's Rocking Chair *

6104 B

Lady's Rocking Chair *

6105 B

Lady's Rocking Chair *

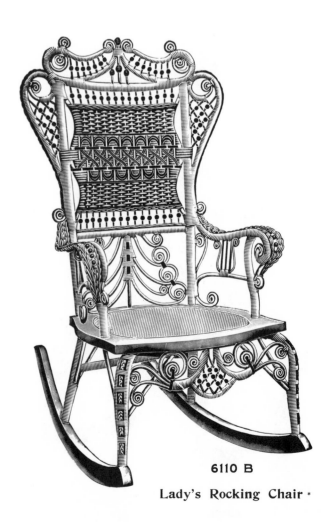

6110 B

Lady's Rocking Chair *

6050 B

Lady's Rocking Chair *

6112 B

Lady's Rocking Chair

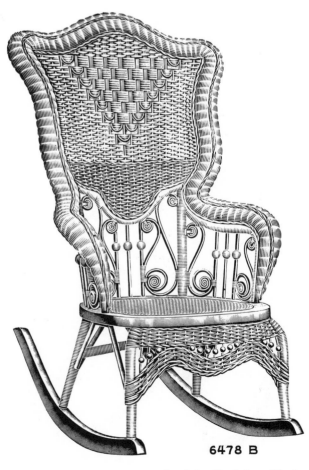

6478 B

Lady's Rocking Chair

6479 B

Lady's Rocking Chair *

6122 B

Lady's Arm Rocking Chair *

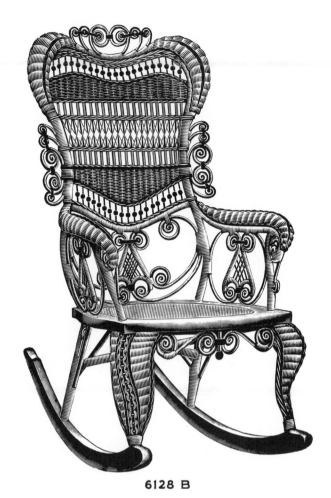

6128 B

Lady's Rocking Chair *

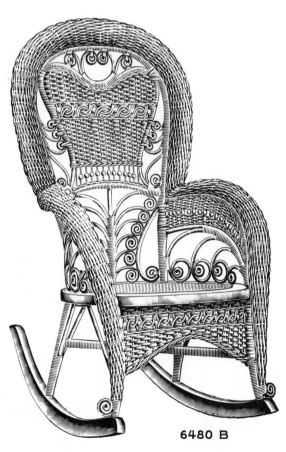

6480 B

Lady's Rocking Chair

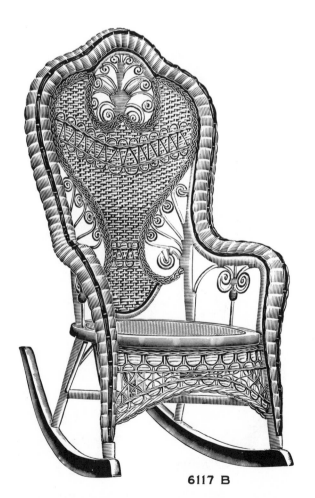

6117 B

Lady's Rocking Chair *

6116 B

Lady's Rocking Chair *

6120 B

Lady's Rocking Chair *

6482 B

Lady's Rocking Chair *

6481 B

Lady's Rocking Chair *

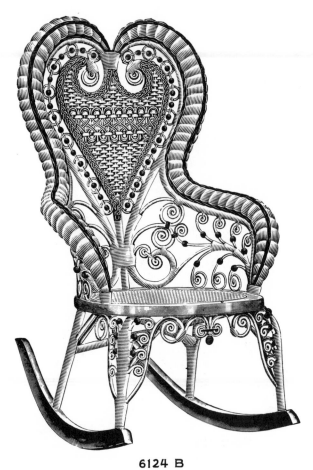

6124 B

Lady's Rocking Chair *

6125 B

Lady's Rocking Chair *

6068 B

Lady's Rocking Chair

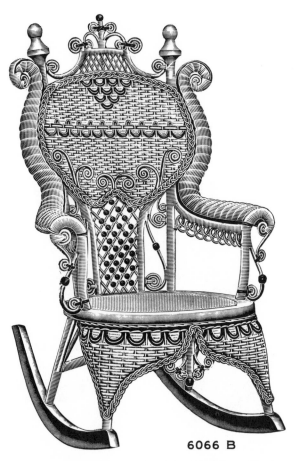

6066 B

Lady's Rocking Chair *

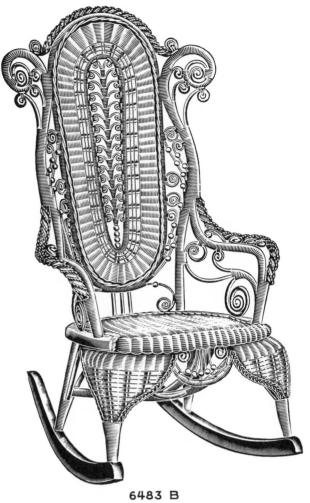

6483 B

Lady's Rocking Chair *

6484 B

Lady's Rocking Chair

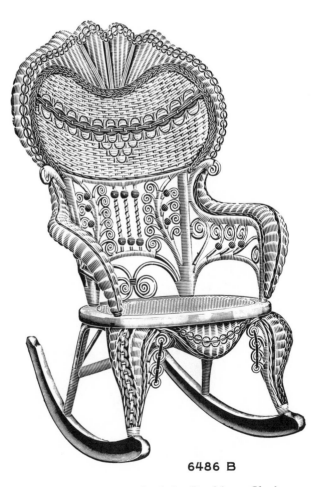

6486 B

Lady's Rocking Chair *

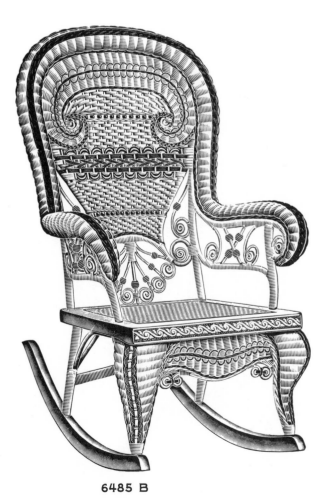

6485 B

Lady's Rocking Chair *

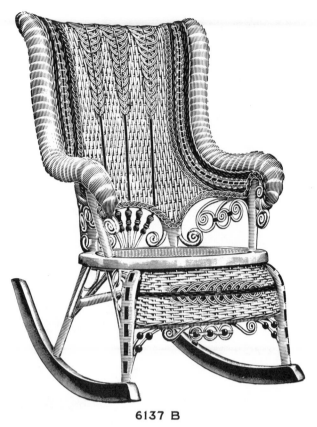

6137 B

Lady's Rocking Chair *

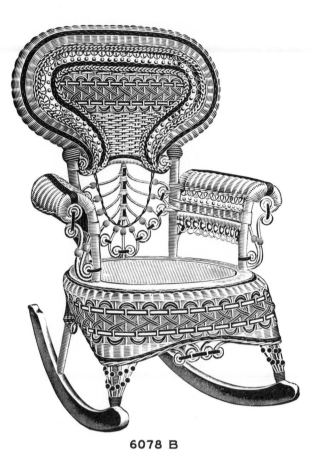

6078 B

Lady's Rocking Chair *

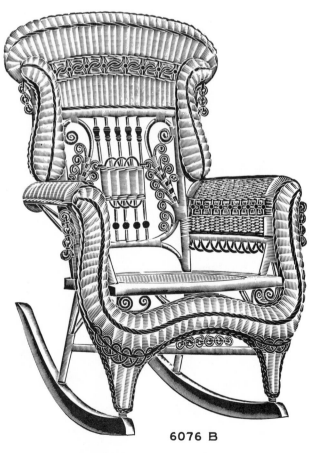

6076 B

Lady's Arm Rocking Chair *

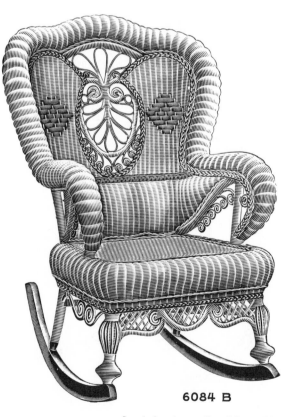

6084 B

Lady's Arm Rocking Chair

6545 A

Lady's Arm Chair

6545 B

Lady's Rocking Chair

6487 B

Lady's Comfort Rocking Chair ·

6488 B

Lady's Comfort Rocking Chair

6149 B

Lady's Comfort Rocking Chair *

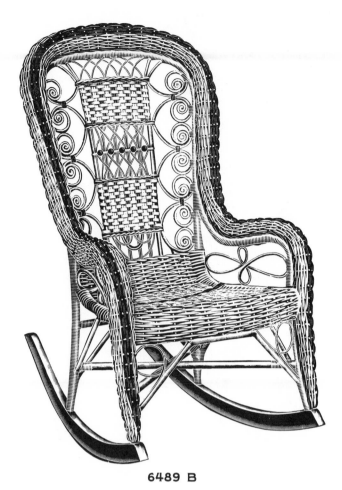

6489 B

Lady's Comfort Rocking Chair *

6156 B

Lady's Comfort Rocking Chair

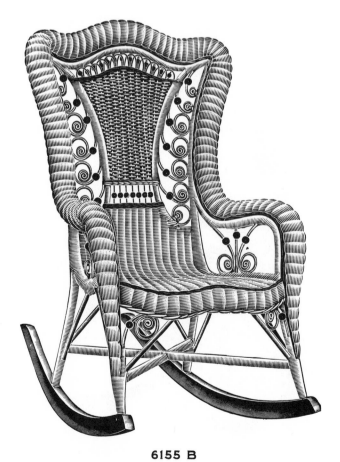

6155 B

Lady's Comfort Rocking Chair *

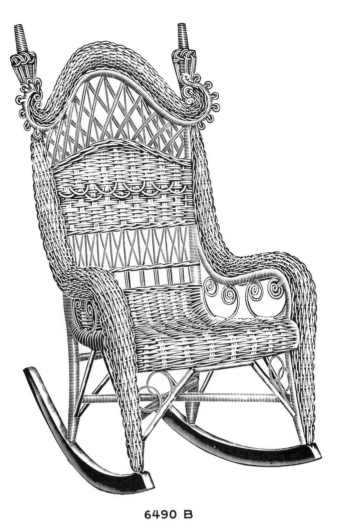

6490 B

Lady's Comfort Rocking Chair

6158 B

Lady's Comfort Rocking Chair

6157 B

Lady's Comfort Rocking Chair *

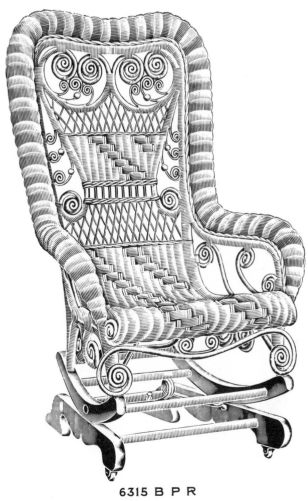

6315 B P R

Lady's Comfort Patent Rocker *

6159 B

Lady's Comfort Rocking Chair

6160 B

Lady's Comfort Rocking Chair

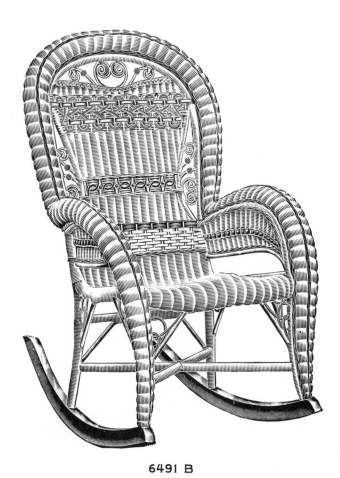

6491 B

Lady's Comfort Rocking Chair ·

6492 B

Lady's Comfort Rocking Chair ·

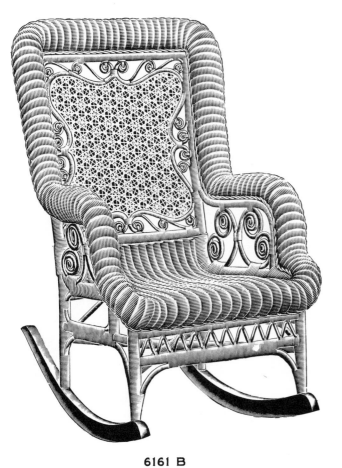

6161 B

Lady's Comfort Rocking Chair

6317 B P R

Lady's Comfort Patent Rocker

6157 D

Large Comfort Rocking Chair *

6164 D

Large Comfort Rocking Chair

6160 D

Large Comfort Rocking Chair

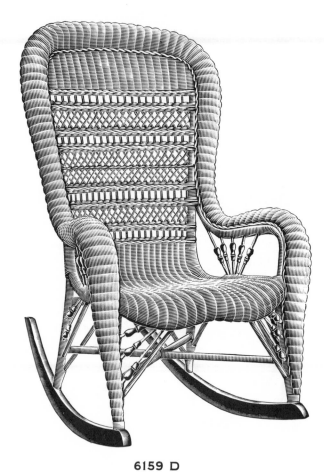

6159 D

Large Comfort Rocking Chair

6167 D

Large Comfort Rocking Chair

6183 D

Large Arm Rocking Chair

6161 D

Large Comfort Rocking Chair

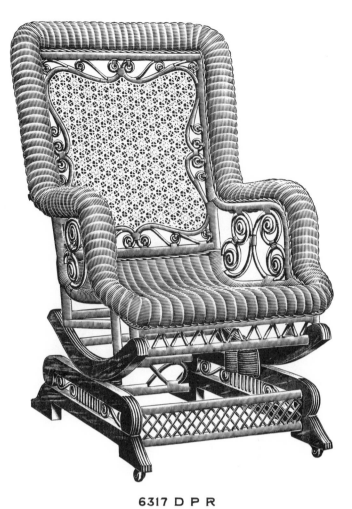

6317 D P R

Large Comfort Patent Rocker

6011 D

Large Arm Rocking Chair

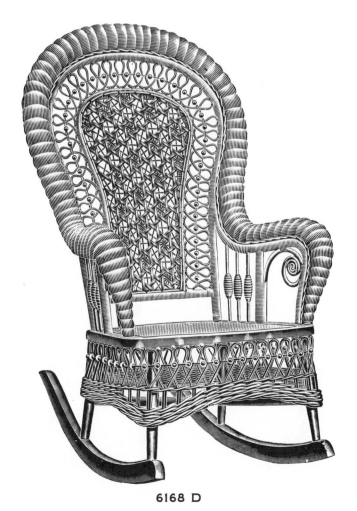

6168 D

Large Arm Rocking Chair

[37 & 38] *19*

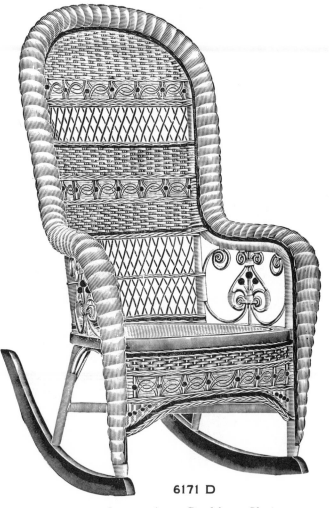

6171 D

Large Arm Rocking Chair *

6172 D

Large Arm Rocking Chair *

6120 D

Large Arm Rocking Chair *

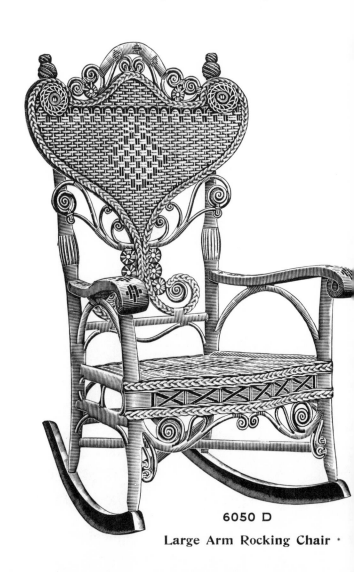

6050 D

Large Arm Rocking Chair *

6177 D

Large Arm Rocking Chair

6184 D

Large Arm Rocking Chair

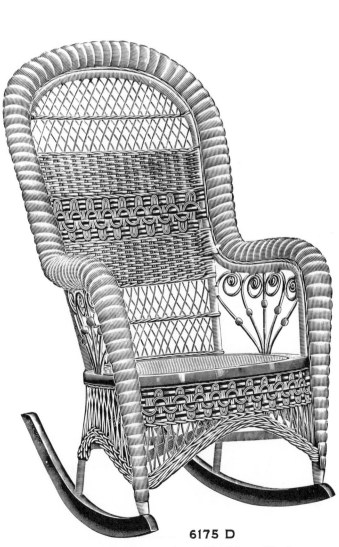

6175 D

Large Arm Rocking Chair *

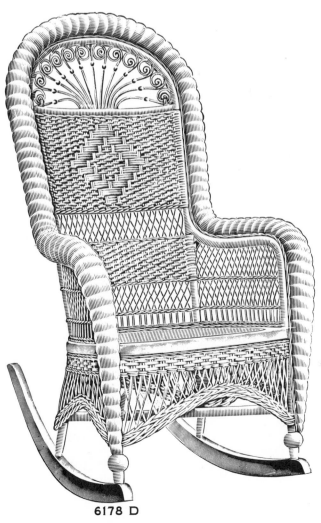

6178 D

Large Arm Rocking Chair

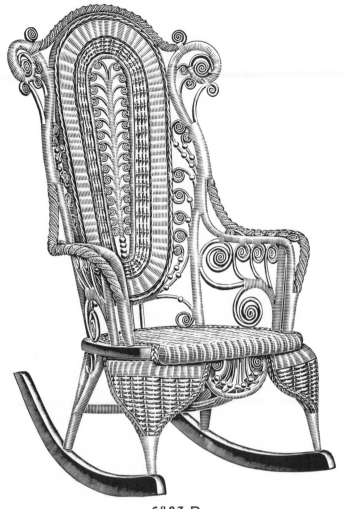

6483 D
Large Arm Rocking Chair *

6068 D
Large Arm Rocking Chair

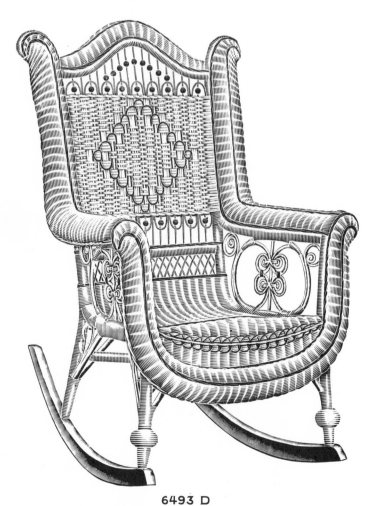

6493 D
Large Arm Rocking Chair *

6066 D
Large Arm Rocking Chair *

6494 D
Large Arm Rocking Chair *

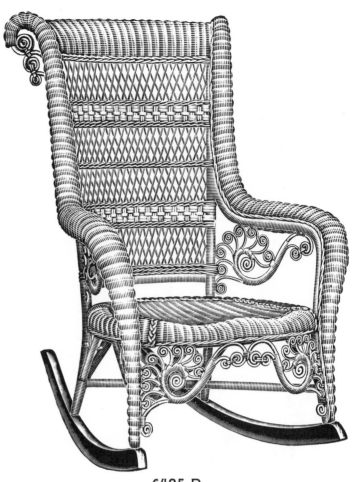

6495 D
Large Arm Rocking Chair

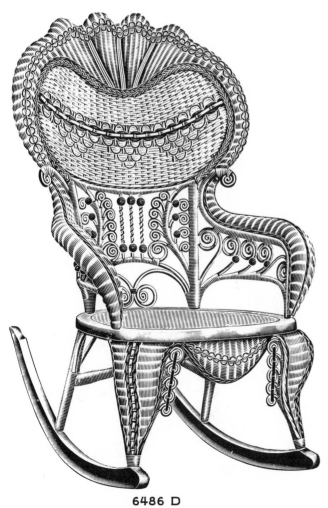

6486 D
Large Arm Rocking Chair *

6193 D
Large Arm Rocking Chair *

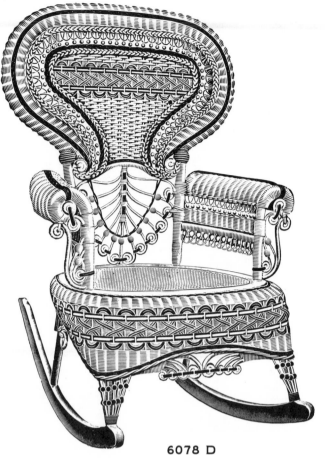

6078 D
Large Arm Rocking Chair *

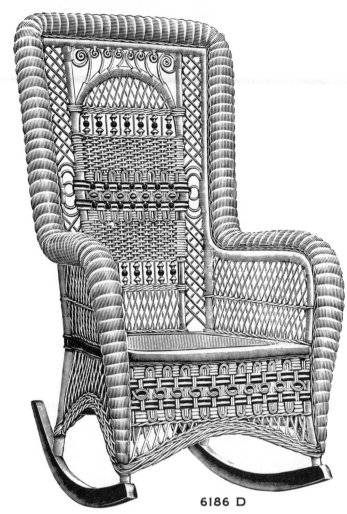

6186 D
Large Arm Rocking Chair *

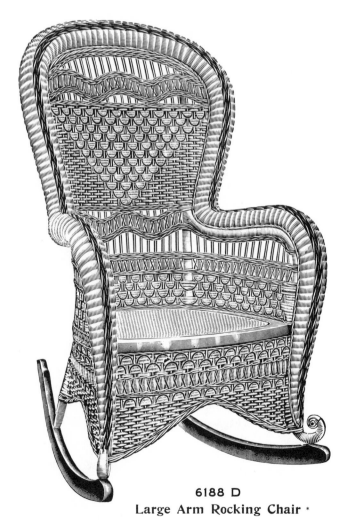

6188 D
Large Arm Rocking Chair *

6076 D
Large Arm Rocking Chair *

6496 D

Large Arm Rocking Chair

6084 D

Large Arm Rocking Chair

6000 A

Lady's Reception Chair *

6003 A

Lady's Reception Chair

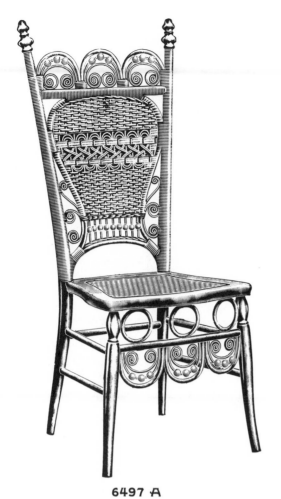

6497 A

Lady's Reception Chair

6006 A

Lady's Reception Chair *

6013 A

Lady's Reception Chair

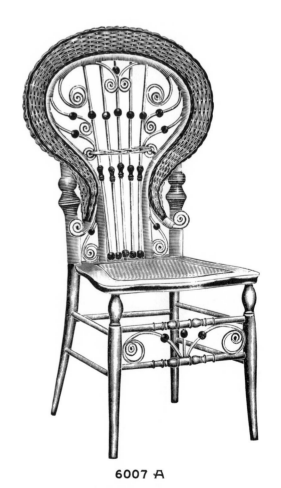

6007 A

Lady's Reception Chair *

6014 A

Lady's Reception Chair *

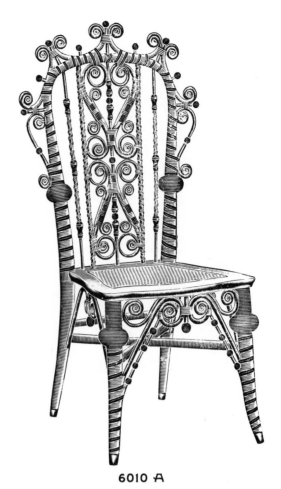

6010 A

Lady's Reception Chair *

6498 A

Lady's Reception Chair

6015 A

Lady's Reception Chair

6021 A

Lady's Reception Chair

6018 A

Lady's Reception Chair *

6023 A

Lady's Reception Chair *

6024 A

Lady's Reception Chair *

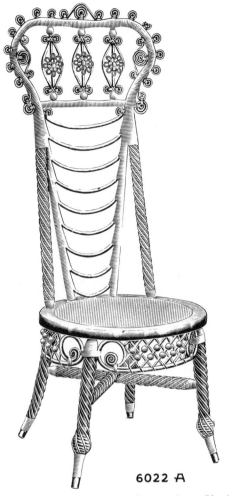

6022 A

Lady's Reception Chair

6500 A

Lady's Reception Chair *

6499 A

Lady's Reception Chair *

6026 A

Lady's Reception Chair *

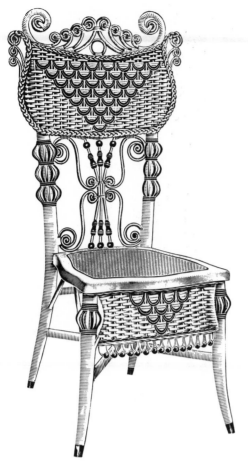

6035 A
Lady's Reception Chair *

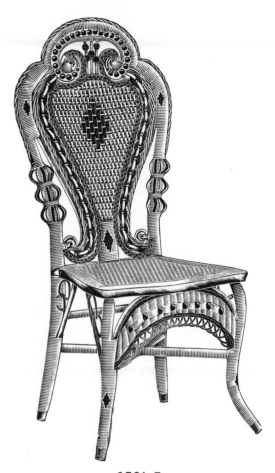

6501 A
Lady's Reception Chair *

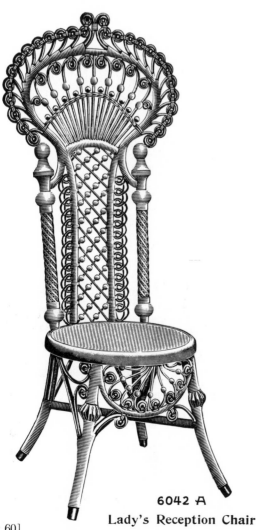

6042 A
Lady's Reception Chair

6502 A
Lady's Reception Chair *

6037 A
Lady's Reception Chair *

6050 A
Lady's Reception Chair *

6039 A
Lady's Reception Chair

6047 A
Lady's Reception Chair *

6011 A

Lady's Arm Chair

6025 A

Lady's Arm Chair

6017 A

Lady's Arm Chair *

6028 A

Lady's Arm Chair

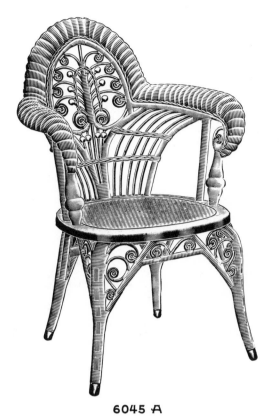

6045 A

Lady's Arm Chair

6041 A

Lady's Arm Chair

6038 A

Lady's Arm Chair *

6046 A

Lady's Arm Chair *

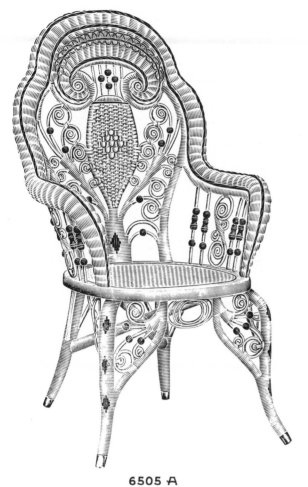

6505 A

Lady's Arm Chair *

6503 A

Lady's Arm Chair *

6055 A

Lady's Arm Chair

6506 A

Lady's Arm Chair

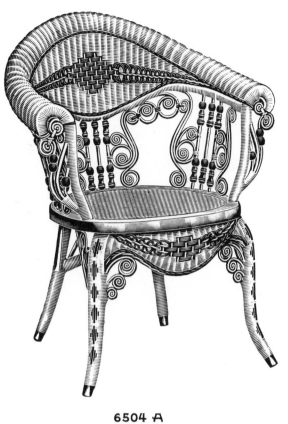

6504 A

Lady's Arm Chair *

6032 A

Lady's Arm Chair *

6062 A

Fancy Reception Chair *

6056 A

Lady's Arm Chair

6061 A

Arm Chair

6060 A

Arm Chair

6482 A

Lady's Arm Chair *

6507 A

Lady's Arm Chair *

6508 A

Lady's Arm Chair

6509 A

Lady's Arm Chair *

6064 A

Arm Chair

6065 A

Arm Chair *

6068 A

Lady's Arm Chair

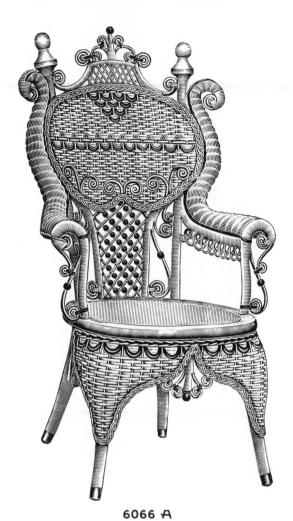

6066 A

Lady's Arm Chair *

6510 A

Lady's Arm Chair *

6511 A

Lady's Arm Chair

6067 A

Arm Chair

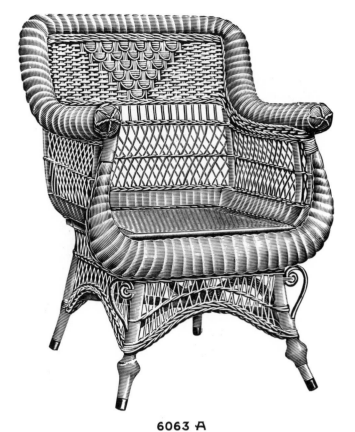

6063 A

Arm Chair

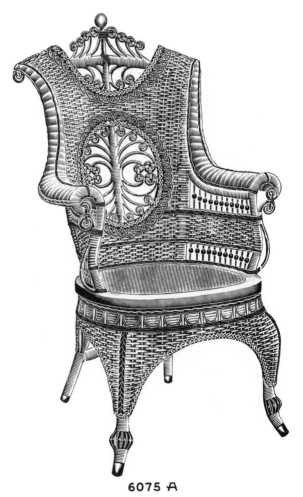

6075 A

Lady's Arm Chair *

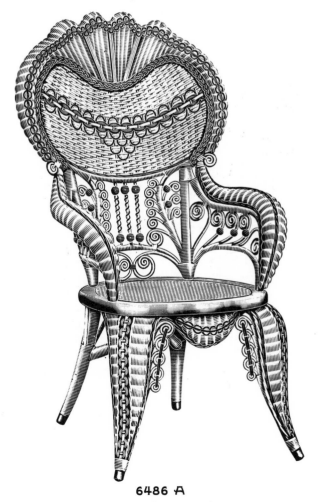

6486 A

Lady's Arm Chair *

6072 A

Lady's Reception Chair *

6074 A

Arm Chair

6515 A

Lady's Arm Chair *

6514 A

Lady's Arm Chair

6078 A
Lady's Arm Chair *

6081 A
Lady's Arm Chair *

6516 A
Lady's Reception Chair *

6076 A
Lady's Arm Chair *

6226 A

Arm Chair

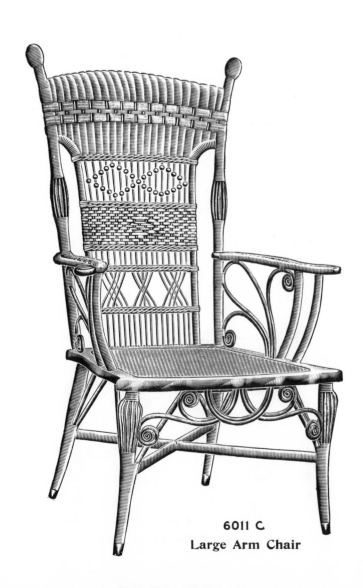

6084 A

Arm Chair

6194 C

Large Arm Chair

6011 C

Large Arm Chair

6195 C
Large Arm Chair

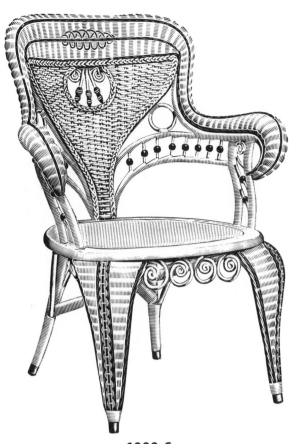

6200 C
Large Arm Chair *

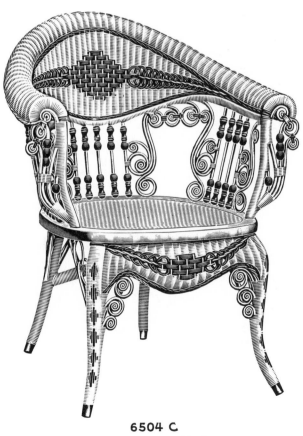

6504 C
Large Arm Chair *

6513 C
Large Arm Chair *

6204 C
Large Arm Chair *

6512 C
Large Arm Chair *

6479 C

Large Arm Chair *

6177 C

Large Arm Chair

6201 C.

Large Arm Chair

6206 C.

Large Arm Chair

6208 C.

Gent's Arm Chair

6207 C.

Large Arm Chair

6212 C.

Large Arm Chair

6213 C.

Large Arm Chair

6137 C.
Large Arm Chair *

6209 C
Large Arm Chair *

6215 C
Gent's Arm Chair

6068 C
Large Arm Chair

6220 C

Large Arm Chair

6219 C

Large Arm Chair

6066 C

Large Arm Chair *

6218 C

Large Arm Chair

6072 C

Large Fancy Chair *

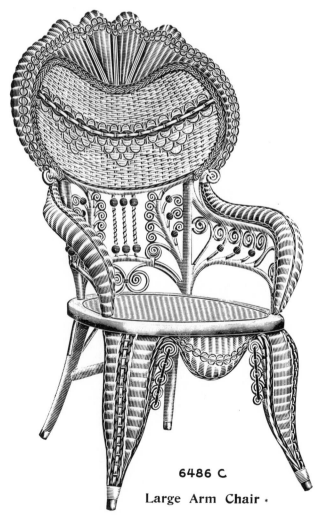

6486 C

Large Arm Chair *

6221 C

Large Arm Chair

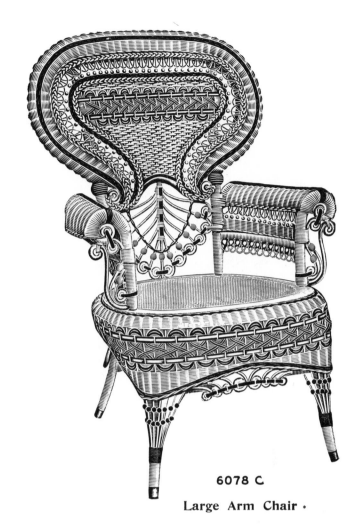

6078 C

Large Arm Chair *

6226 C

Large Arm Chair

6224 C

Extra Large Arm Chair

6084 C.

Large Arm Chair

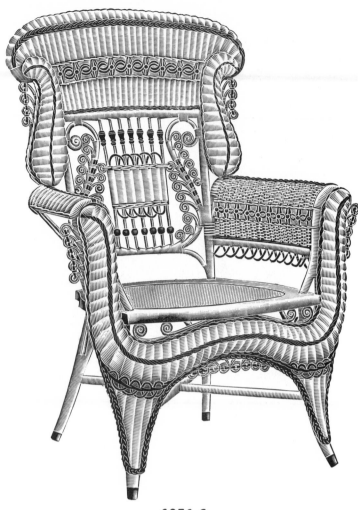

6076 C.

Large Arm Chair ·

6254

Morris Chair

6255

Morris Chair

6521
Morris Chair

6257
Morris Chair *

6522
Morris Chair *

6523
Morris Chair *

6251

Reclining Chair

6259

Conversation Chair

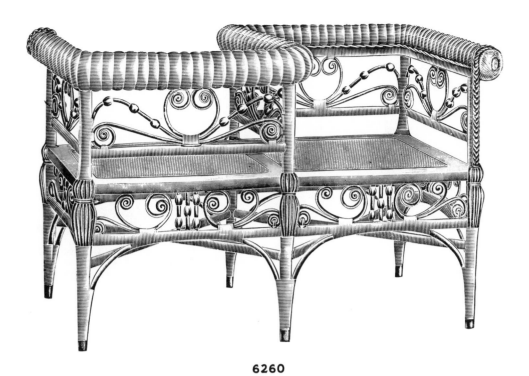

6260

Conversation Chair

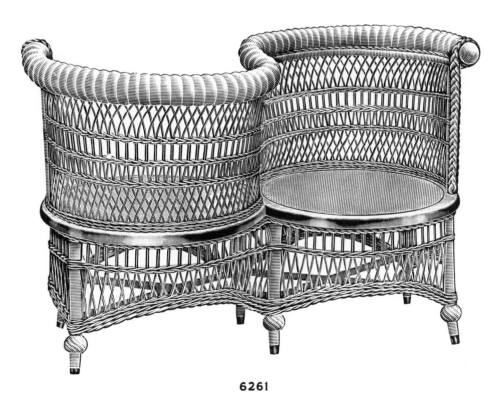

6261

Conversation Chair

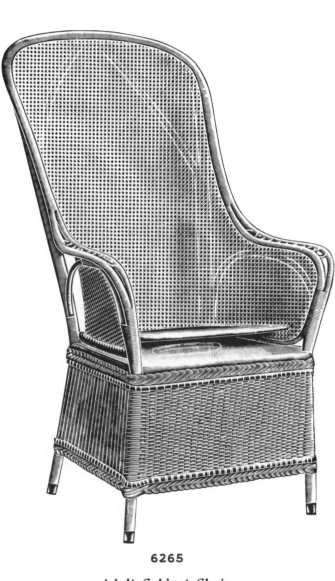

6265

Adult Cabinet Chair

6264

Beach Chair

6262

Conversation Chair

6321

Corner Chair

6322

Corner Chair

6324

Fancy Reception Chair ·

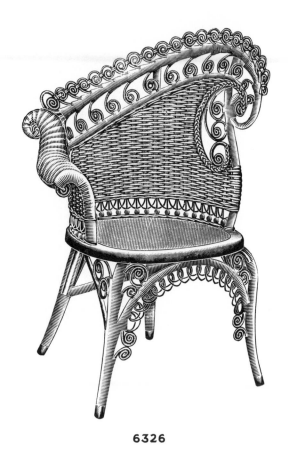

6326

Fancy Reception Chair

6331

Fancy Reception Chair

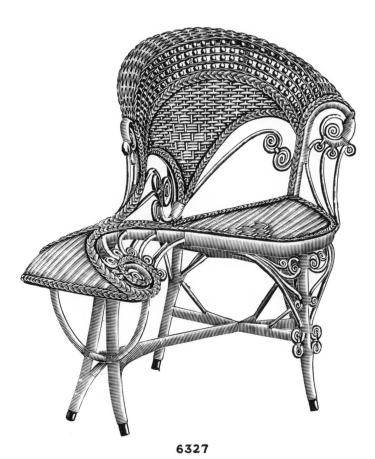

6327

Fancy Chair

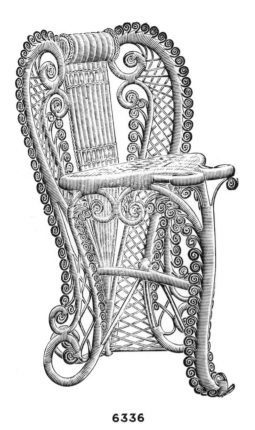

6336

Posing Chair—Front View

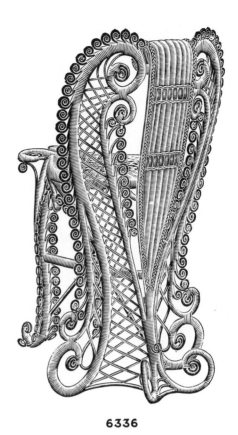

6336

Posing Chair—Rear View

6332

Fancy Reception Chair

6338

Fancy Reception Chair

6337

Fancy Reception Chair

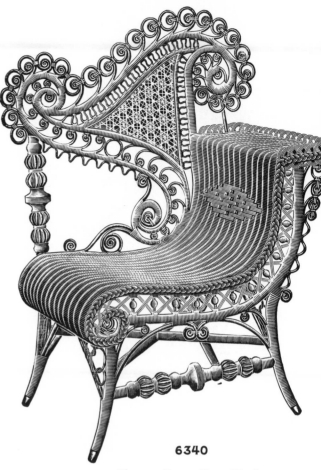

6340

Fancy Reception Chair

6369

Piano Stool

6370

Piano Chair

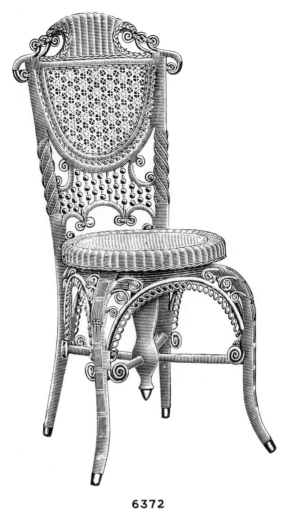

6372

Piano Chair

6371

Piano Chair

6364

Turkish Chair

6320

Turkish Chair

6319

Turkish Chair

6325

Turkish Chair

6334

Turkish Chair

6339

Turkish Chair *

6517

Divan *

6343

Divan

6347

Divan *

6342

Divan *

6518 *

Divan

6519 *

Divan

6520

Divan *

6351

Divan

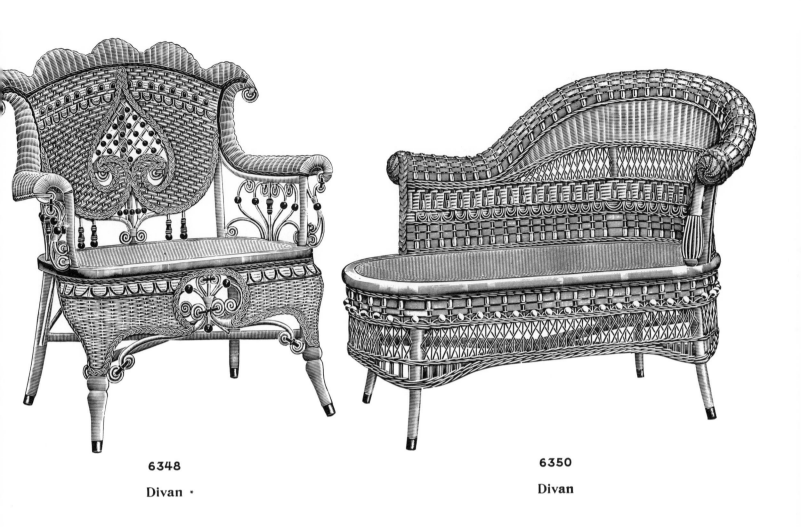

6348

Divan *

6350

Divan

6229 F

Tete-a-Tete

6479 F

Tete-a-Tete .

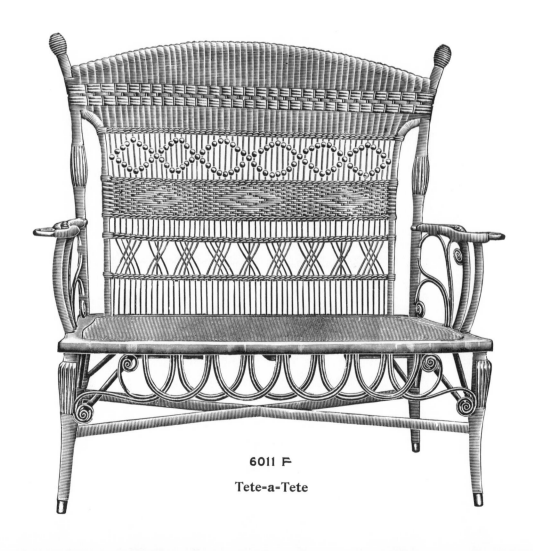

6011 F

Tete-a-Tete

6482 F

Tete-a-Tete .

6230 F

Tete-a-Tete

6504 F

Tete=a=Tete *

6066 F

Tete=a=Tete *

6068 F
Tete-a-Tete

6078 F
Tete-a-Tete *

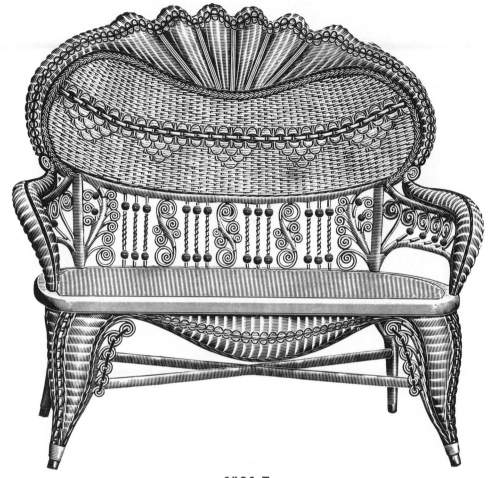

6486 F
Tete=a=Tete *

6072 F
Tete=a=Tete *

6076 F
Tete=a=Tete

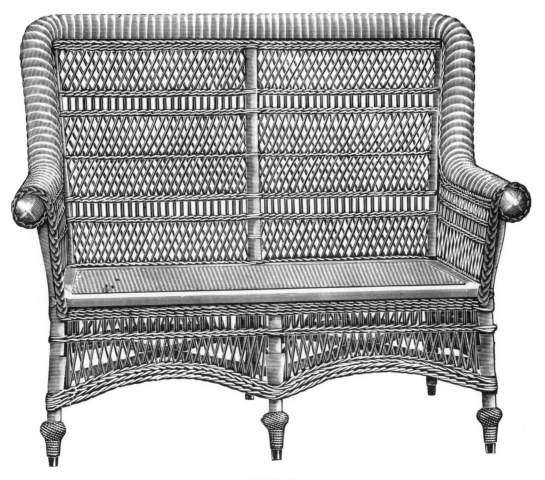

6231 F

Tete=a=Tete

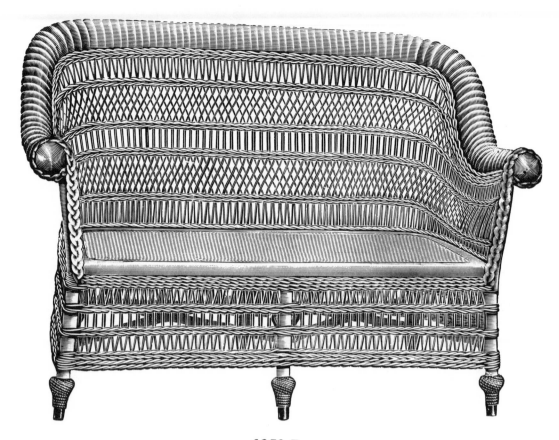

6232 F

Tete-a-Tete

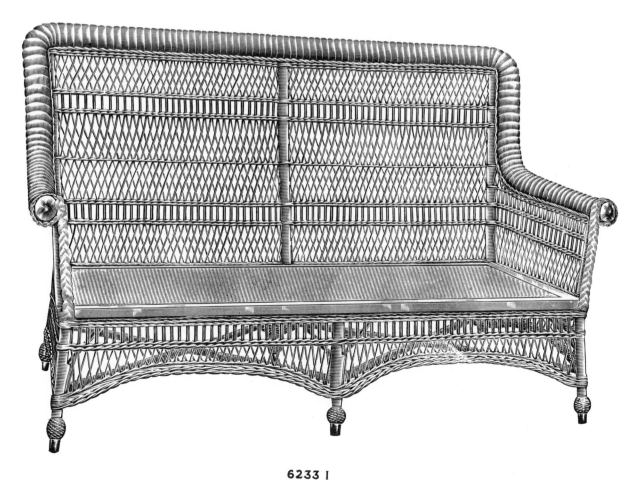

6233 I

Extra Long Sofa

6084 F

Tete-a-Tete

6234

Couch

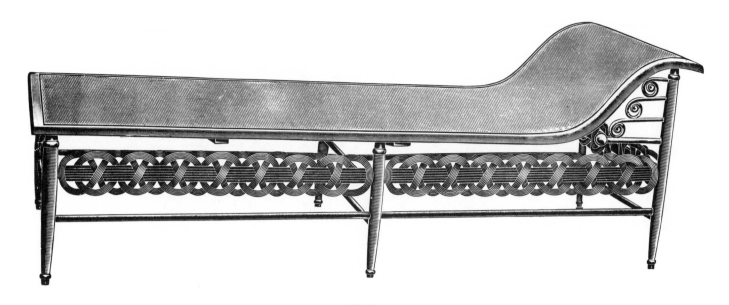

6235

Couch

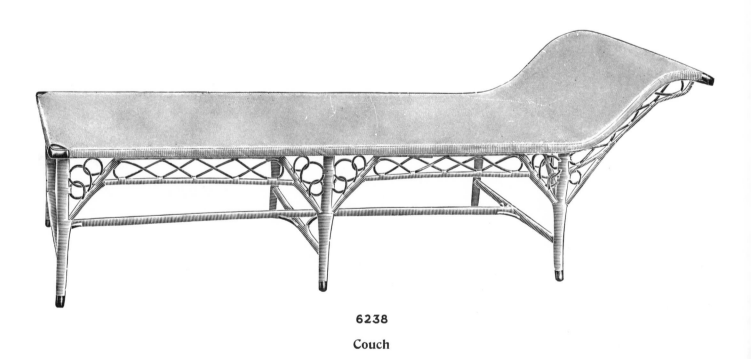

6238

Couch

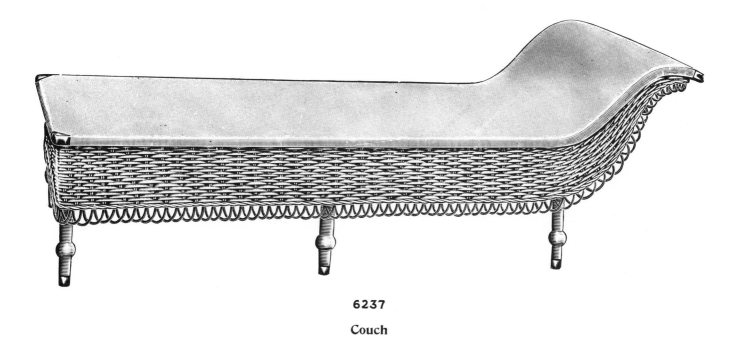

6237

Couch

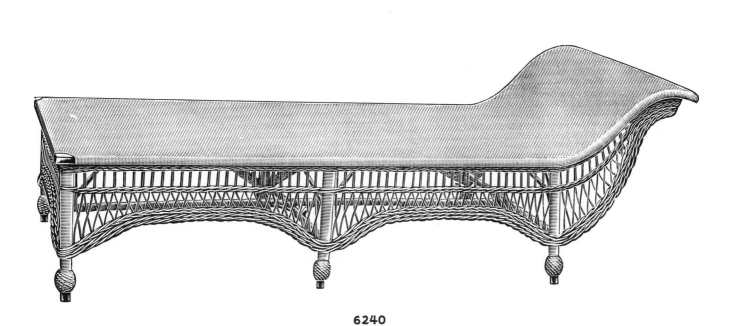

6240

Couch

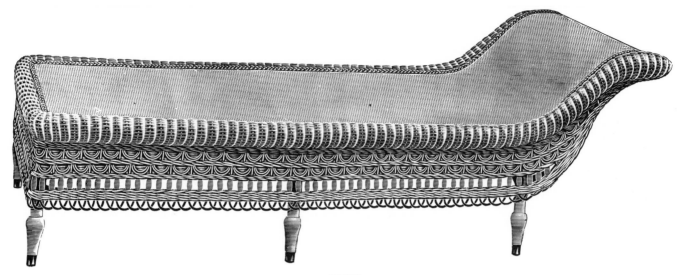

6242

Couch

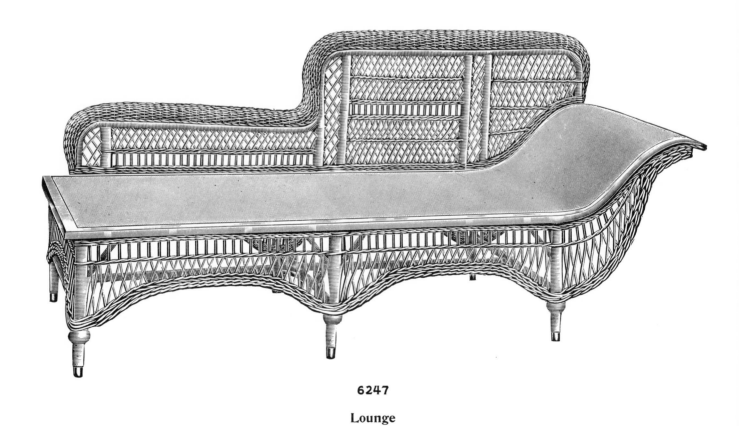

6247

Lounge

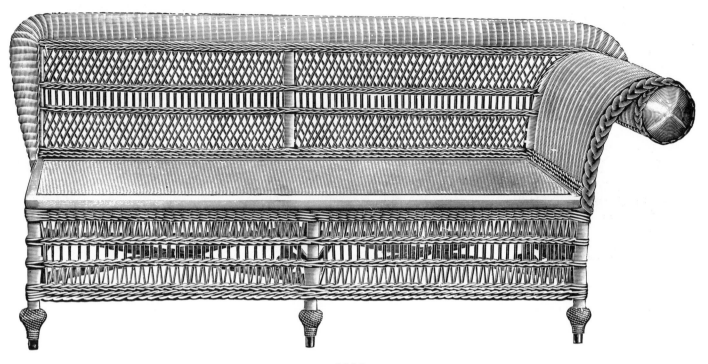

6248

Lounge

6266

Child's Cabinet Chair

6267

Child's Cabinet Chair

6268

Child's Cabinet Chair

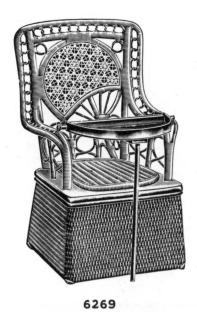

6269

Child's Cabinet Chair

6280

Child's Rocking Chair

6279

Child's Chair

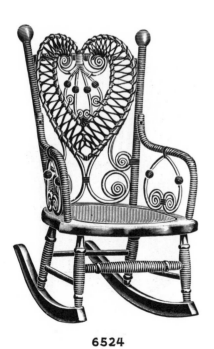

6524

Child's Rocking Chair ·

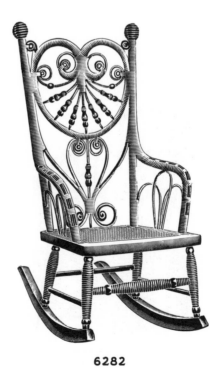

6282

Child's Rocking Chair ·

6283

Child's Rocking Chair ·

6289

Child's Comfort Rocker

6284

Child's Comfort Rocker ·

6285

Child's Rocking Chair ·

6526

Child's Rocking Chair ·

6286

Child's Rocking Chair ·

6525

Child's Rocking Chair ·

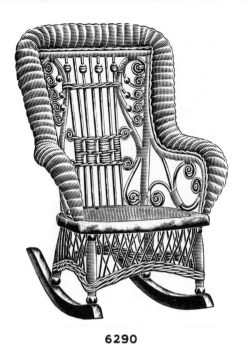

6290

Child's Rocking Chair

6287

Child's Rocking Chair *

6297

Child's Rocking Chair *

6527

Child's Rocking Chair *

6528

Child's Rocking Chair *

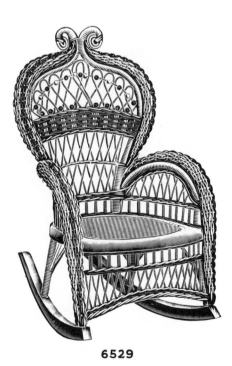

6529

Child's Rocking Chair *

6530

Child's Rocking Chair *

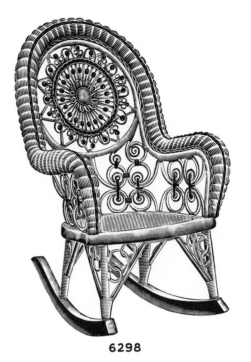

6298

Child's Rocking Chair *

6299

Child's Rocking Chair *

6532

Child's Rocking Chair *

6300

Child's Chair

6301

Child's Rocking Chair

6280½ S

Child's Table Chair, with Shelf

6302½ S

Child's Table Chair, with Shelf

6303½ S

Child's Table Chair, with Shelf

6282½ S

Child's Table Chair, with Shelf *

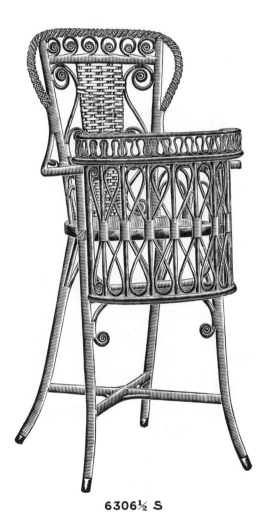

6306½ S

Child's Table Chair, with Shelf

6292½ S

Child's Table Chair, with Shelf

6309½ S

Child's Table Chair, with Shelf

6310½ S

Child's Table Chair, with Shelf

6312

Misses' Comfort Rocker

6311

Misses' Comfort Rocker

6313

Misses' Comfort Rocker *

6531

Misses' Comfort Rocker *

6270

Bassinet

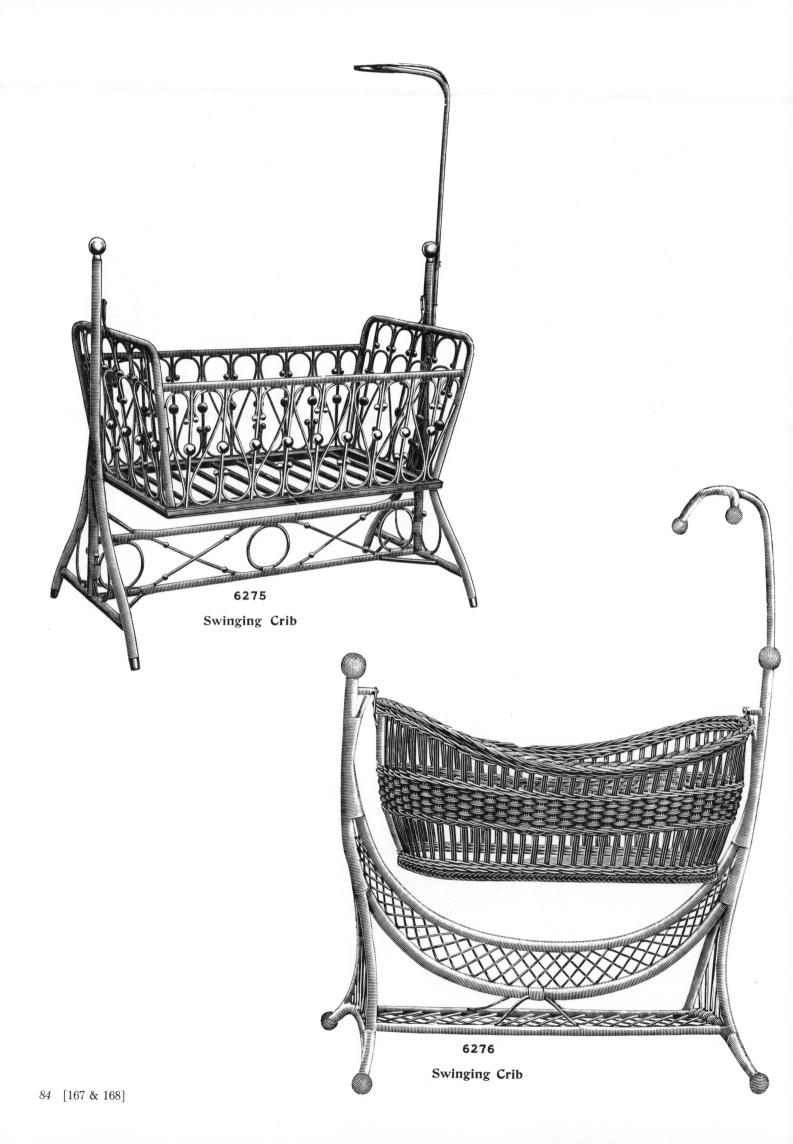

6275

Swinging Crib

6276

Swinging Crib

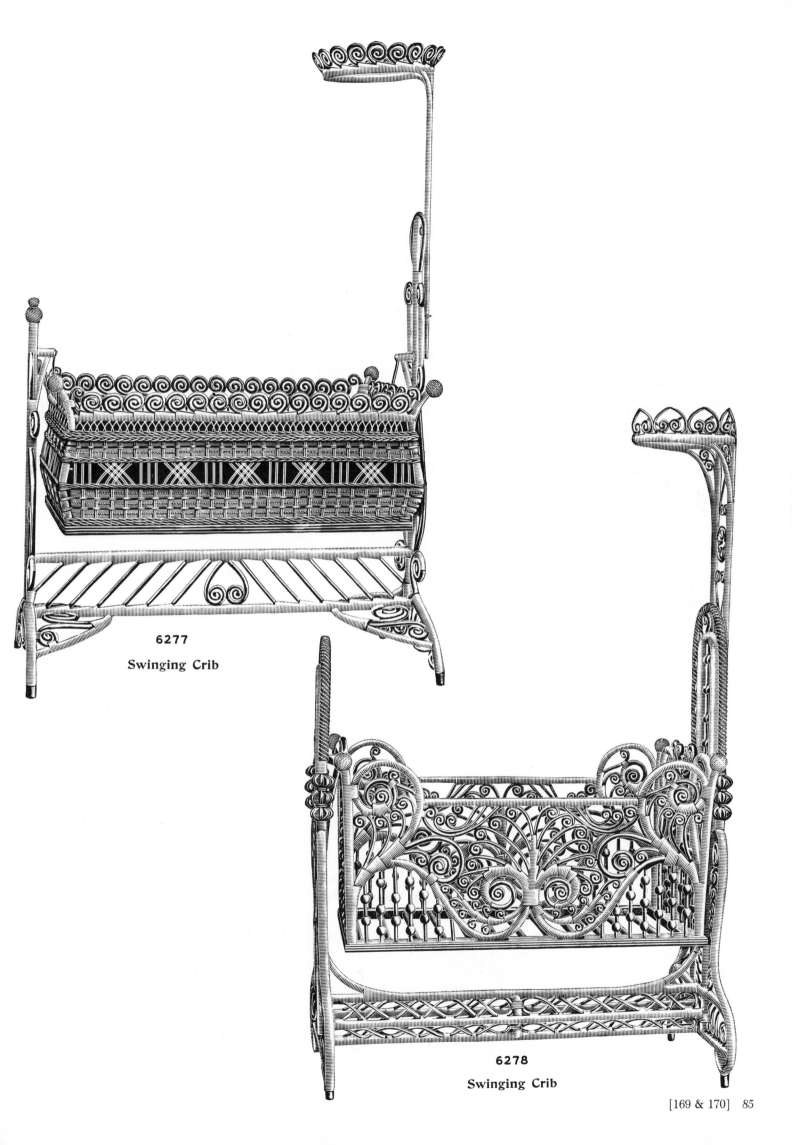

6277

Swinging Crib

6278

Swinging Crib

6271

Standing Crib—Drop Side

6272

Standing Crib—Drop Side

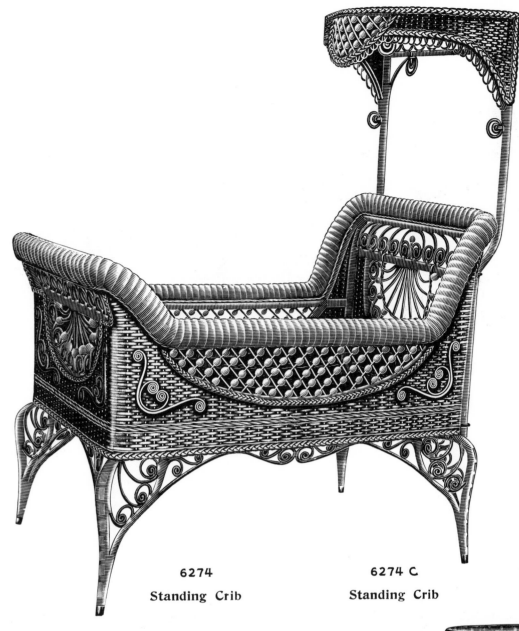

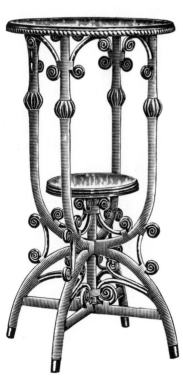

6274
Standing Crib

6274 C
Standing Crib

6377
Round Table

6380
Round Table

6381
Round Stand

6383

Round Table

6385

Round Table

6384

Oblong Table

6389

Oblong Table

6388

Oblong Table

6397

Round Table

6394

Oblong Table

6404

Round Table

6538

Square Table ·

6539

Oblong Table

6408

Round Table ·

6407

Round Table ·

6409

Round Table ·

6411

Square Table *

6415

Square Table

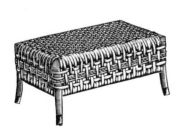

6355

Oblong Cricket

6354

Round Cricket

6357

Ottoman

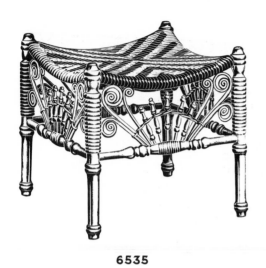

6535

Ottoman *

6358

Ottoman

6361

Ottoman *

6362

Ottoman

6536

Ottoman *

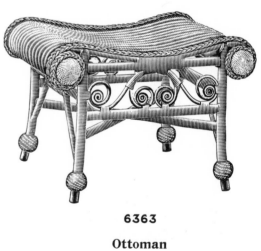

6363

Ottoman

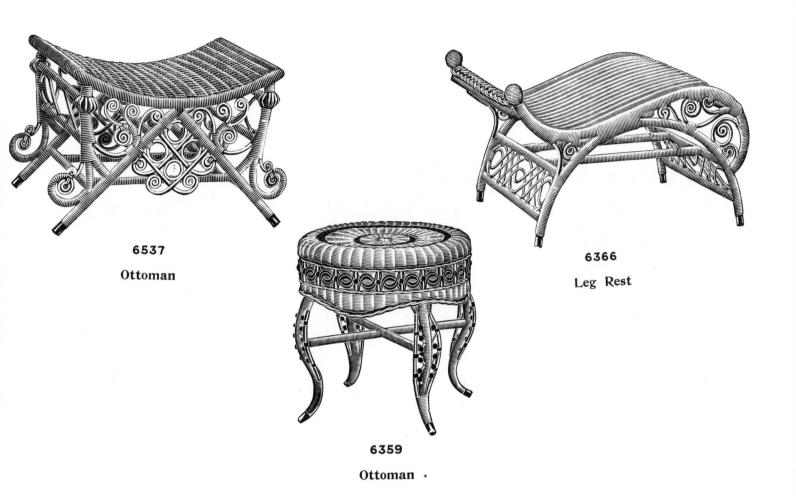

6537

Ottoman

6366

Leg Rest

6359

Ottoman *

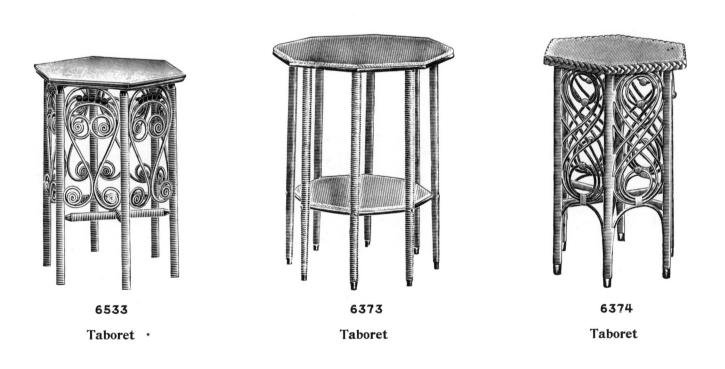

6533

Taboret *

6373

Taboret

6374

Taboret

6375

Taboret

6376

Taboret ·

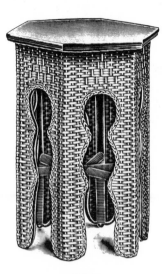

6534

Taboret

6540

Jardiniere ·

6541

Jardiniere ·

6542

Jardiniere ·

6432

Jardiniere *

6434

Jardiniere *

6435

Jardiniere *

6546

Fancy Office Baskets

6551

Carpet Beater

6547

Woven Office Baskets

6550

Covered Laundry Baskets

6549

Square Hamper

6548

Round Hamper

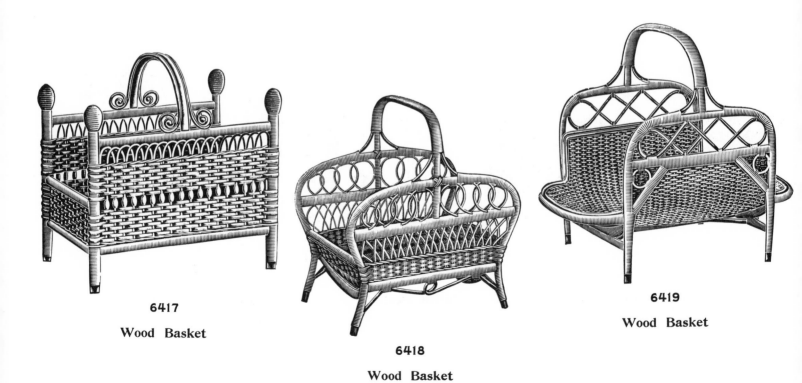

6417

Wood Basket

6418

Wood Basket

6419

Wood Basket

6416

Dog Basket

6360

Ottoman and Hamper

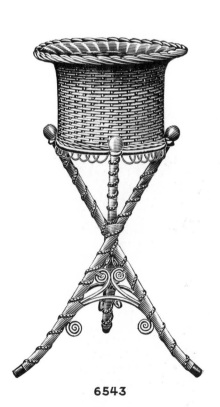

6543

Round Work Basket

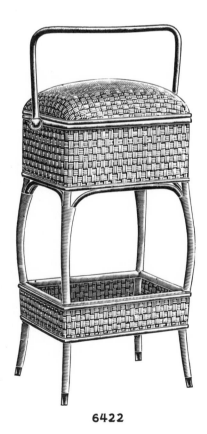

6422

Oblong Work Basket

6421

Oblong Work Basket

6420

Oblong Work Basket

6423

Oblong Work Basket

6424

Oblong Work Basket

6426

Oblong Work Basket

6427

Oblong Work Basket

6544

Fancy Work Basket •

6431

Oblong Work Basket

6436

Music Stand

6438

Music Stand

6437

Music Stand •

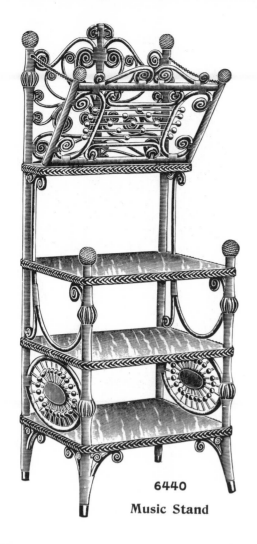

6440

Music Stand

6442

Bric-a-Brac Stand

6443

Fancy Cabinet

6444

Fancy Cabinet

6445

Dressing Stand

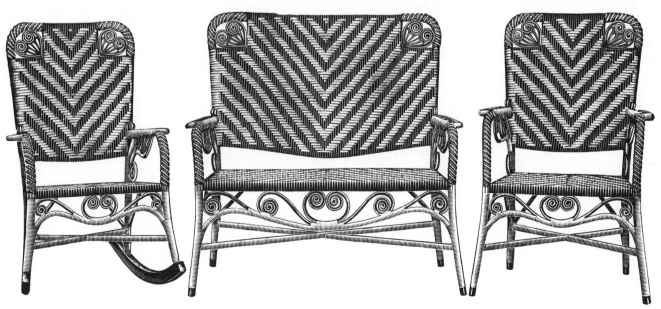

| 6479 B | 6479 F | 6479 C |

6479 Suite—Three Pieces

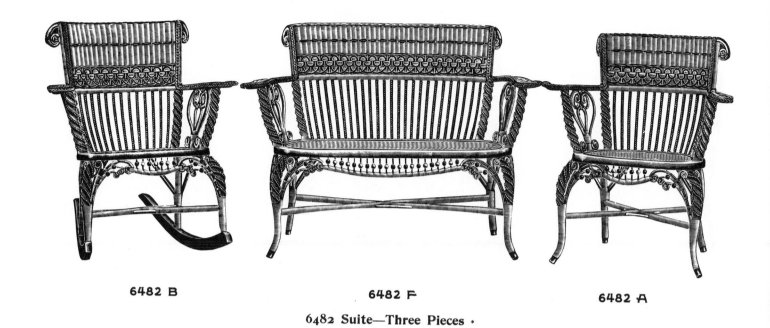

6482 B　　　　　　　　**6482 F**　　　　　　　　**6482 A**

6482 Suite—Three Pieces ·

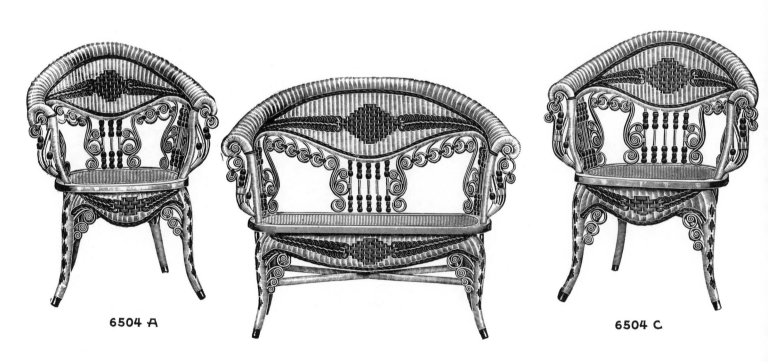

6504 A　　　　　　　　　　　　　　　　　**6504 C**

6504 F

6504 Suite—Three Pieces ·

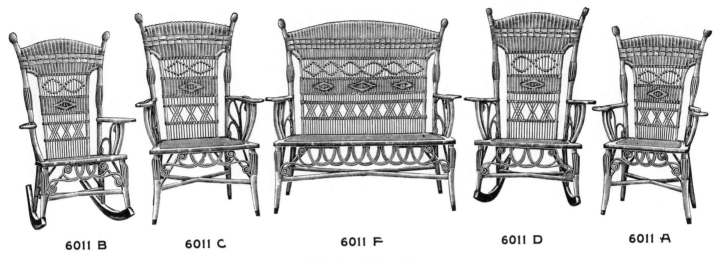

6011 B   **6011 C**   **6011 F**   **6011 D**   **6011 A**

6011 Suite—Five Pieces

6072 C   **6072 F**   **6072 A**

6072 Suite—Three Pieces *

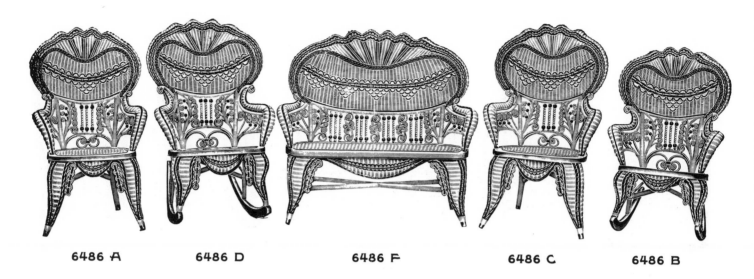

| 6486 A | 6486 D | 6486 F | 6486 C | 6486 B |

6486 Suite—Five Pieces *

| 6066 B | 6066 C | 6066 F | 6066 D | 6066 A |

6066 Suite—Five Pieces *

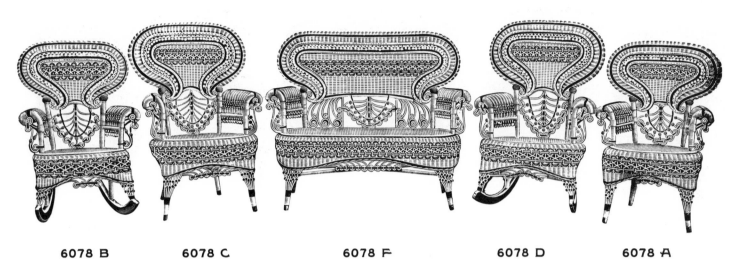

6078 B   6078 C   6078 F   6078 D   6078 A

6078 Suite—Five Pieces *

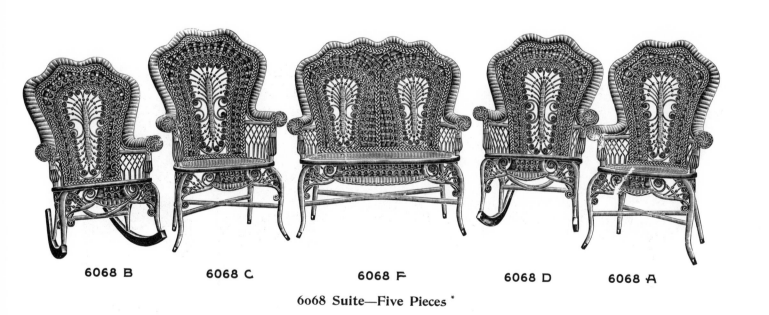

6068 B   6068 C   6068 F   6068 D   6068 A

6068 Suite—Five Pieces *

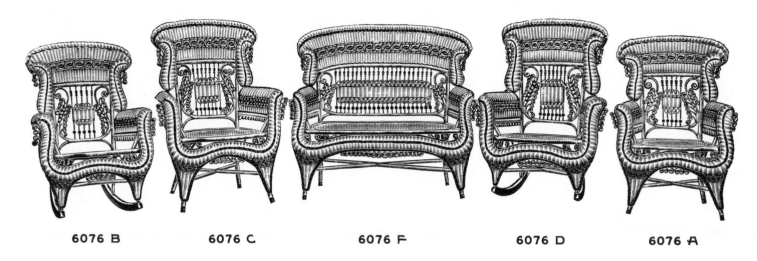

6076 B   **6076 C**   **6076 F**   **6076 D**   **6076 A**

6076 Suite—Five Pieces *

6084 C   **6084 B**   **6084 F**   **6084 A**   **6084 D**

6084 Suite—Five Pieces

THE END